CORNERSTONES
for Living

Tyndale House Publishers, Inc.
WHEATON, ILLINOIS

Visit Tyndale's exciting Web site at www.tyndale.com

Cornerstones for Living © 1997 by Tyndale House Publishers, Inc. All rights reserved.

The Cornerstones notes were adapted from the *New Believer's Bible* reading tracks, copyright © 1996 by Greg Laurie. All rights reserved.

Scripture passages are taken from the *Holy Bible*, New Living Translation, copyright © 1996 by Tyndale Charitable Trust. All rights reserved.

The text of the *Holy Bible*, New Living Translation, may be quoted in any form (written, visual, electronic, or audio) up to and inclusive of two hundred fifty (250) verses without express written permission of the publisher, provided that the verses quoted do not account for more than 20 percent of the work in which they are quoted, and provided that a complete book of the Bible is not quoted. When the *Holy Bible*, New Living Translation, is quoted, the following credit line must appear on the copyright page or title page of the work:

Scripture quotations are taken from the *Holy Bible*, New Living Translation, copyright © 1996. Used by permission of Tyndale House Publishers, Inc., Wheaton, Illinois 60189. All rights reserved.

When quotations from the NLT text are used in nonsalable media, such as church bulletins, orders of service, newsletters, transparencies, or similar media, a complete copyright notice is not required, but the initials (NLT) must appear at the end of each quotation.

Quotations in excess of two hundred fifty (250) verses or 20 percent of the work, or other permission requests, must be directed to and approved in writing by Tyndale House Publishers, Inc., P.O. Box 80, Wheaton, Illinois 60189.

New Living, *NLT*, and the New Living Translation logo are trademarks of Tyndale House Publishers, Inc.

ISBN 0-8423-3399-1

Printed in the United States of America

02	01	00	99	98	97	
8	7	6	5	4	3	2

Each sale of the *Holy Bible*, New Living Translation, benefits Wycliffe Bible Translators, which completed its four hundredth New Testament in 1995 and is currently working in another one thousand languages. Tyndale House Publishers and Wycliffe Bible Translators share the vision for an understandable, accurate translation of the Bible for every person.

CONTENTS

A Note to Readers

With 40 million copies in print, *The Living Bible* has been meeting a great need in people's hearts for more than thirty years. But even good things can be improved, so ninety evangelical scholars from various theological backgrounds and denominations were commissioned in 1989 to begin revising *The Living Bible*. The end result of this seven-year process is the *Holy Bible*, New Living Translation—a general-purpose translation that is accurate, easy to read, and excellent for study.

The goal of any Bible translation is to convey the meaning of the ancient Hebrew and Greek texts as accurately as possible to the modern reader. The New Living Translation is based on the most recent scholarship in the theory of translation. The challenge for the translators was to create a text that would make the same impact in the life of modern readers that the original text had for the original readers. In the New Living Translation, this is accomplished by translating entire thoughts (rather than just words) into natural, everyday English. The end result is a translation that is easy to read and understand and that accurately communicates the meaning of the original text.

We believe that this new translation, which combines the latest in scholarship with the best in translation style, will speak to your heart. We present the New Living Translation with the prayer that God will use it to speak his timeless truth to the church and to the world in a fresh, new way.

The Publishers
July 1996

Preface: Cornerstones for Living

A solid block of stone—a cornerstone—was traditionally used to start any new building's foundation. It was a strong, stable base upon which the building could stand firm. Without such a foundation, the building would sink, shift, and soon crumble. Our life, like a building, needs a solid foundation to build upon. Without a reliable foundation, we will be crushed by the storms of life, like a beach shanty in a hurricane.

Jesus once said, "Anyone who listens to my teaching and obeys me is wise, like a person who builds a house on solid rock. Though the rain comes in torrents and the floodwaters rise and the winds beat against that house, it won't collapse, because it is built on rock. But anyone who hears my teaching and ignores it is foolish, like a person who builds a house on sand. When the rains and floods come and the winds beat against that house, it will fall with a mighty crash" (Matthew 7:24-27).

The "cornerstones" in this book—passages from God's Word, the Bible—will help you lay a solid foundation for your life. Here you will learn about the character of God, the person of Jesus Christ, and the Holy Spirit's work in the lives of believers. You will learn what the Bible says about Satan, heaven, and hell. You will also discover important character traits that are developed and nurtured by a personal relationship with God. Some of these are love, joy, peace, and purity. Each of these "cornerstones for living" will be illuminated by several passages from the *Holy Bible*,

New Living Translation. A short note will follow each passage to drive home its important life-giving message. May God bless you as you seek to build a solid foundation for your life.

Who Is God?

Thousands of years ago, the pharaoh, ruler of Egypt, posed a question people are still asking today: "Who is God that I should obey him?" That's a good question, but it is not an easy subject to tackle. It is difficult for our limited mind to grasp the limitless, eternal God. It has been said, "If God were small enough for your mind, he wouldn't be big enough for your needs." For that reason, we shouldn't be exasperated if we cannot fully understand who God is or why he does certain things. One day, Scripture promises, everything about God and his character will be made perfectly clear to us (1 Corinthians 13:12). But until then, we will find everything we need to know about him in his Word.

God Is All-Knowing and Ever-Present
PSALM 139:1-24
For the choir director: A psalm of David.

¹ O LORD, you have examined my heart
     and know everything about me.
² You know when I sit down or stand up.

1

You know my every thought when far away.
³You chart the path ahead of me
    and tell me where to stop and rest.
    Every moment you know where I am.
⁴You know what I am going to say
    even before I say it, LORD.
⁵You both precede and follow me.
    You place your hand of blessing on my head.
⁶Such knowledge is too wonderful for me,
    too great for me to know!

⁷I can never escape from your spirit!
    I can never get away from your presence!
⁸If I go up to heaven, you are there;
    if I go down to the place of the dead,* you are there.
⁹If I ride the wings of the morning,
    if I dwell by the farthest oceans,
¹⁰even there your hand will guide me,
    and your strength will support me.
¹¹I could ask the darkness to hide me
    and the light around me to become night—
¹²but even in darkness I cannot hide from you.
    To you the night shines as bright as day.
    Darkness and light are both alike to you.

¹³You made all the delicate, inner parts of my body
    and knit me together in my mother's womb.
¹⁴Thank you for making me so wonderfully complex!
    Your workmanship is marvelous—and how well
        I know it.
¹⁵You watched me as I was being formed in utter
    seclusion,
    as I was woven together in the dark of the womb.

139:8 Hebrew *to Sheol.*

2

¹⁶You saw me before I was born.
   Every day of my life was recorded in your book.
   Every moment was laid out
   before a single day had passed.

¹⁷How precious are your thoughts about me,* O God!
   They are innumerable!
¹⁸I can't even count them;
   they outnumber the grains of sand!
   And when I wake up in the morning,
   you are still with me!

¹⁹O God, if only you would destroy the wicked!
   Get out of my life, you murderers!
²⁰They blaspheme you;
   your enemies take your name in vain.
²¹O LORD, shouldn't I hate those who hate you?
   Shouldn't I despise those who resist you?
²²Yes, I hate them with complete hatred,
   for your enemies are my enemies.

²³Search me, O God, and know my heart;
   test me and know my thoughts.
²⁴Point out anything in me that offends you,
   and lead me along the path of everlasting life.

139:17 Or *How precious to me are your thoughts.*

INSIGHTS FOR LIFE:
Scripture teaches us about many of God's characteristics. This psalm highlights two of them. First, God is all-knowing. As verses 1-6 attest, God knows every detail about what is going on in his amazing and complex creation. If God pays that much attention to detail, we can be assured that he is always aware of what is happening in our life. Second, verses 7-12 show us that God is ever-present. There is no place the psalmist

can go to escape the presence of God. This brings comfort to those who need God's present help but equal discomfort to those who have reason to hide from God. God's presence should not only bring us comfort but also motivate us to live a life pleasing to him.

God Is Powerful and Personal
ACTS 17:22-34

[22]So Paul, standing before the Council,* addressed them as follows: "Men of Athens, I notice that you are very religious, [23]for as I was walking along I saw your many altars. And one of them had this inscription on it—'To an Unknown God.' You have been worshiping him without knowing who he is, and now I wish to tell you about him.

[24]"He is the God who made the world and everything in it. Since he is Lord of heaven and earth, he doesn't live in man-made temples, [25]and human hands can't serve his needs—for he has no needs. He himself gives life and breath to everything, and he satisfies every need there is. [26]From one man he created all the nations throughout the whole earth. He decided beforehand which should rise and fall, and he determined their boundaries.

[27]"His purpose in all of this was that the nations should seek after God and perhaps feel their way toward him and find him—though he is not far from any one of us. [28]For in him we live and move and exist. As one of your own poets says, 'We are his offspring.' [29]And since this is true, we shouldn't think of God as an idol designed by craftsmen from gold or silver or stone. [30]God overlooked people's former ignorance about these things, but now he commands every-

17:22 Or *in the middle of Mars Hill*; Greek reads *in the middle of the Areopagus*.

4

one everywhere to turn away from idols and turn to him.* ³¹For he has set a day for judging the world with justice by the man he has appointed, and he proved to everyone who this is by raising him from the dead."

³²When they heard Paul speak of the resurrection of a person who had been dead, some laughed, but others said, "We want to hear more about this later." ³³That ended Paul's discussion with them, ³⁴but some joined him and became believers. Among them were Dionysius, a member of the Council,* a woman named Damaris, and others.

17:30 Greek *everywhere to repent.*   17:34 Greek *an Areopagite.*

INSIGHTS FOR LIFE:
Paul's audience in this passage included people of two different beliefs. There were those who did not believe in life after death and lived only for pleasure (the Epicureans). There were also those who believed that God existed in every material object and who sought to be at peace with the world around them (the Stoics). In speaking to these two groups, Paul showed them how their philosophies fell short of grasping the true nature of God. He did this by explaining first that God as the all-powerful Creator. But then he revealed that God is not just an impersonal force but a person deeply concerned about maintaining intimate relationships with the people he created. We can be thankful that the true God not only created us but also sustains, loves, and desires an intimate relationship with us.

God Is Loving and Just
2 PETER 3:3-10

³First, I want to remind you that in the last days there will be scoffers who will laugh at the truth and do every evil thing they desire. ⁴This will be their argument: "Jesus prom-

ised to come back, did he? Then where is he? Why, as far back as anyone can remember, everything has remained exactly the same since the world was first created."

⁵They deliberately forget that God made the heavens by the word of his command, and he brought the earth up from the water and surrounded it with water. ⁶Then he used the water to destroy the world with a mighty flood. ⁷And God has also commanded that the heavens and the earth will be consumed by fire on the day of judgment, when ungodly people will perish.

⁸But you must not forget, dear friends, that a day is like a thousand years to the Lord, and a thousand years is like a day. ⁹The Lord isn't really being slow about his promise to return, as some people think. No, he is being patient for your sake. He does not want anyone to perish, so he is giving more time for everyone to repent. ¹⁰But the day of the Lord will come as unexpectedly as thief. Then the heavens will pass away with a terrible noise, and everything in them will disappear in fire, and the earth and everything on it will be exposed to judgment.*

3:10 Some manuscripts read *will be burned up.*

INSIGHTS FOR LIFE:
This passage shows two important and seemingly contra-dictory aspects of God's character: love and justice. The Bible tells us that God is loving. Despite God's knowledge of our sin, he reached out to offer us forgiveness through the death of his Son on the cross. But God's love is often misunder-stood. Many think that because he loves us, he will overlook our sins. But the fact that God is loving does not negate the fact that he is also just. Scripture repeatedly makes the point that only the godly will see God's face. We can be certain

that our sins must be dealt with, either by accepting God's gift of salvation through faith or by suffering God's ultimate judgment. The choice is ours to make, and God desires that all would receive his forgiveness.

Who Is Jesus?

Throughout history people have tried to answer this question. Our best source for finding an answer to this question is God's own Word. The Bible presents us with some inescapable truths about Jesus that demand a response. Anyone who seriously studies Scripture to learn more about Jesus must answer two probing questions: What do you think of Jesus Christ? and Who is he? Writer C. S. Lewis made this observation: "You must make your choice. Either this man was and is the Son of God, or else he is a madman or something worse. You can shut him up for a fool, you can spit at him and kill him as a demon, or you can fall at his feet and call him Lord and God. But let us not come with any patronizing nonsense about his being a great human teacher. He has not left that open to us. He did not intend to" (*Mere Christianity,* bk. II, chapter three, pp. 55–56). Jesus was not just a good man. He was—and is—the God-man.

Jesus Is Divine
COLOSSIANS 1:15-23

[15]Christ is the visible image of the invisible God. He existed before God made anything at all and is supreme

over all creation.* ¹⁶Christ is the one through whom God created everything in heaven and earth. He made the things we can see and the things we can't see—kings, kingdoms, rulers, and authorities. Everything has been created through him and for him. ¹⁷He existed before everything else began, and he holds all creation together.

¹⁸Christ is the head of the church, which is his body. He is the first of all who will rise from the dead,* so he is first in everything. ¹⁹For God in all his fullness was pleased to live in Christ, ²⁰and by him God reconciled everything to himself. He made peace with everything in heaven and on earth by means of his blood on the cross. ²¹This includes you who were once so far away from God. You were his enemies, separated from him by your evil thoughts and actions, ²²yet now he has brought you back as his friends. He has done this through his death on the cross in his own human body. As a result, he has brought you into the very presence of God, and you are holy and blameless as you stand before him without a single fault. ²³But you must continue to believe this truth and stand in it firmly. Don't drift away from the assurance you received when you heard the Good News. The Good News has been preached all over the world, and I, Paul, have been appointed by God to proclaim it.

1:15 Greek *He is the firstborn of all creation.*   1:18 Greek *He is the beginning, the firstborn from the dead.*

INSIGHTS FOR LIFE:
The most crucial truth of the Christian faith is that Jesus Christ, though he came to earth as a man, was in fact God. Several statements in this passage point to the divinity of Jesus. First, he is eternal, existing before the creation of the world (verse 15). Second, Jesus is the Creator of all things (verse 16). Third, Jesus not only created everything, he also

holds it all together (verses 16-17). Fourth, Jesus is the head of the church, the group of true believers (verse 18). Fifth, Jesus was the first to defeat death and return to life (verse 18), giving us hope that we, too, will one day rise from the dead. Finally, Jesus, as God, has brought peace between his broken and sinful creation and holy God (verse 20).

Jesus Is Human

PHILIPPIANS 2:3-11

³Don't be selfish; don't live to make a good impression on others. Be humble, thinking of others as better than yourself. ⁴Don't think only about your own affairs, but be interested in others, too, and what they are doing.

⁵Your attitude should be the same that Christ Jesus had. ⁶Though he was God, he did not demand and cling to his rights as God. ⁷He made himself nothing;* he took the humble position of a slave and appeared in human form.* ⁸And in human form he obediently humbled himself even further by dying a criminal's death on a cross. ⁹Because of this, God raised him up to the heights of heaven and gave him a name that is above every other name, ¹⁰so that at the name of Jesus every knee will bow, in heaven and on earth and under the earth, ¹¹and every tongue will confess that Jesus Christ is Lord, to the glory of God the Father.

2:7a Or *He laid aside his mighty power and glory.* 2:7b Greek *and was born in the likeness of men and was found in appearance as a man.*

INSIGHTS FOR LIFE:

Jesus became our supreme example as God in human form. He took the disguise of a slave, emptying himself of his privileges as God. Jesus—God in human form—experienced hunger. He endured sorrow. He grew tired. He felt the sting of loneliness. He felt the pressure of temptation. For these reasons, we can be assured that God understands what we are going through in life. But we can be thankful that Jesus was not just a man. He was able to rise above human circumstances to reconcile sinful people to a holy God. At the end of time, every knee will bow and every tongue will confess that Jesus Christ is Lord. Christ's divine nature, which he veiled at times during his time on earth, will then be clearly visible for all to see.

Jesus Made the Ultimate Sacrifice
ISAIAH 53:1-12

¹Who has believed our message? To whom will the LORD reveal his saving power? ²My servant grew up in the LORD's presence like a tender green shoot, sprouting from a root in dry and sterile ground. There was nothing beautiful or majestic about his appearance, nothing to attract us to him. ³He was despised and rejected—a man of sorrows, acquainted with bitterest grief. We turned our backs on him and looked the other way when he went by. He was despised, and we did not care.

⁴Yet it was our weaknesses he carried; it was our sorrows* that weighed him down. And we thought his troubles were a punishment from God for his own sins! ⁵But he was wounded and crushed for our sins. He was beaten that we might have peace. He was whipped, and we were healed! ⁶All of us have strayed away like sheep. We have left God's paths to follow our own. Yet the LORD laid on him the guilt and sins of us all.

⁷He was oppressed and treated harshly, yet he never said a word. He was led as a lamb to the slaughter. And as a sheep is silent before the shearers, he did not open his mouth. ⁸From prison and trial they led him away to his

53:4 Or *Yet it was our sicknesses he carried; it was our diseases.*

death. But who among the people realized that he was dying for their sins—that he was suffering their punishment? ⁹He had done no wrong, and he never deceived anyone. But he was buried like a criminal; he was put in a rich man's grave.

¹⁰But it was the LORD's good plan to crush him and fill him with grief. Yet when his life is made an offering for sin, he will have a multitude of children, many heirs. He will enjoy a long life, and the LORD's plan will prosper in his hands. ¹¹When he sees all that is accomplished by his anguish, he will be satisfied. And because of what he has experienced, my righteous servant will make it possible for many to be counted righteous, for he will bear all their sins. ¹²I will give him the honors of one who is mighty and great, because he exposed himself to death. He was counted among those who were sinners. He bore the sins of many and interceded for sinners.

INSIGHTS FOR LIFE:

Death on the cross was not a rude interruption of the otherwise wonderful ministry of a great teacher. Jesus chose to take the punishment for our sins because he knew that there was no other way for us to approach a holy God. The fact that Jesus knew what awaited him at the cross makes his journey to earth even more amazing. Christ's terrible death on the cross reveals the depth of our sin; it was a punishment that we deserved. It also demonstrates God's overwhelming love for us; our sin drove in the nails, but his love for us kept him on the cross. If there had been any other way for us to be forgiven, Jesus surely would have found it. But Jesus was willing to suffer this agonizing death for our salvation.

Who Is the Holy Spirit?

The Holy Spirit is the most mysterious member of the Trinity, which includes God the Father, God the Son (Jesus Christ), and God the Holy Spirit. Many struggle with the idea of God being three persons, yet one. Quite honestly, we will never fully grasp the concept this side of heaven. Some have wrongly thought of the Holy Spirit as an impersonal force rather than a person. Perhaps this comes from descriptions of him being like the wind or coming upon Jesus in the form of a dove. Yet these are simply metaphors used in Scripture to help communicate something of God's character. Similarly, Jesus described himself as "the bread of life" and "the Good Shepherd." Jesus said of the Holy Spirit: "When the Spirit of truth comes, he will guide you into all truth. . . . He will tell you about the future" (John 16:13). Note the use of the pronoun *he*. The Holy Spirit has a distinct personality, and he has specific work that he wants to do in our life.

Why God Gives Us the Holy Spirit
EPHESIANS 1:9-14

⁹God's secret plan has now been revealed to us; it is a plan centered on Christ, designed long ago according to his good pleasure. ¹⁰And this is his plan: At the right time he will bring

13

everything together under the authority of Christ—everything in heaven and on earth. [11]Furthermore, because of Christ, we have received an inheritance from God,* for he chose us from the beginning, and all things happen just as he decided long ago. [12]God's purpose was that we who were the first to trust in Christ should praise our glorious God. [13]And now you also have heard the truth, the Good News that God saves you. And when you believed in Christ, he identified you as his own by giving you the Holy Spirit, whom he promised long ago. [14]The Spirit is God's guarantee that he will give us everything he promised and that he has purchased us to be his own people. This is just one more reason for us to praise our glorious God.

1:11 Or *we have become God's inheritance.*

INSIGHTS FOR LIFE:
You might say that the Holy Spirit is our "identifying mark" as believers in Christ. In verses 13-14 we see three reasons why God gives us his Holy Spirit: First, God had promised to send the Holy Spirit to those who trusted Jesus Christ as Savior. Second, the Holy Spirit serves as a mark of ownership, showing that we belong to God. Third, the Holy Spirit represents God's guarantee or pledge to bring us to our final spiritual inheritance. This word translated "guarantee" could also be translated "first installment," signifying that this is just a small portion of what is awaiting us in heaven. God gives us the Holy Spirit not only to enable us to live out the Christian life but to prove that we are precious in his sight.

How the Holy Spirit Works in Our Life
JOHN 14:12-21
[12]"The truth is, anyone who believes in me will do the same works I have done, and even greater works, because I

am going to be with the Father. ¹³You can ask for anything in my name, and I will do it, because the work of the Son brings glory to the Father. ¹⁴Yes, ask anything in my name, and I will do it!

¹⁵"If you love me, obey my commandments. ¹⁶And I will ask the Father, and he will give you another Counselor,* who will never leave you. ¹⁷He is the Holy Spirit, who leads into all truth. The world at large cannot receive him, because it isn't looking for him and doesn't recognize him. But you do, because he lives with you now and later will be in you. ¹⁸No, I will not abandon you as orphans—I will come to you. ¹⁹In just a little while the world will not see me again, but you will. For I will live again, and you will, too. ²⁰When I am raised to life again, you will know that I am in my Father, and you are in me, and I am in you. ²¹Those who obey my commandments are the ones who love me. And because they love me, my Father will love them, and I will love them. And I will reveal myself to each one of them."

14:16 Or *Comforter,* or *Encourager,* or *Advocate.* Greek *Paraclete;* also in 14:26.

INSIGHTS FOR LIFE:
The New Testament uses three Greek prepositions to describe how the Holy Spirit works in our life. Verse 17 shows two of these ways, and a third can be found elsewhere in Scripture. First, he works <u>with</u> (para) us as nonbelievers. Before coming to belief in Jesus Christ, the Holy Spirit convicts us of our sin and reveals Christ as the answer. Second, he comes <u>into</u> (en) our life when we turn to Christ. Once we accept Jesus Christ as our Savior and invite him into our life, the Holy Spirit moves into our life and sets up residence. Third, he comes <u>upon</u> (epi) us to empower us as believers. This aspect of the Holy Spirit's work is described in Luke 24:49, where Jesus says, "And now I will send the Holy Spirit, just as my Father promised."

Why We Need the Holy Spirit

GALATIANS 5:16-26

[16]So I advise you to live according to your new life in the Holy Spirit. Then you won't be doing what your sinful nature craves. [17]The old sinful nature loves to do evil, which is just opposite from what the Holy Spirit wants. And the Spirit gives us desires that are opposite from what the sinful nature desires. These two forces are constantly fighting each other, and your choices are never free from this conflict. [18]But when you are directed by the Holy Spirit, you are no longer subject to the law.

[19]When you follow the desires of your sinful nature, your lives will produce these evil results: sexual immorality, impure thoughts, eagerness for lustful pleasure, [20]idolatry, participation in demonic activities, hostility, quarreling, jealousy, outbursts of anger, selfish ambition, divisions, the feeling that everyone is wrong except those in your own little group, [21]envy, drunkenness, wild parties, and other kinds of sin. Let me tell you again, as I have before, that anyone living that sort of life will not inherit the Kingdom of God.

[22]But when the Holy Spirit controls our lives, he will produce this kind of fruit in us: love, joy, peace, patience, kindness, goodness, faithfulness, [23]gentleness, and self-control. Here there is no conflict with the law.

[24]Those who belong to Christ Jesus have nailed the passions and desires of their sinful nature to his cross and crucified them there. [25]If we are living now by the Holy Spirit, let us follow the Holy Spirit's leading in every part of our lives. [26]Let us not become conceited, or irritate one another, or be jealous of one another.

Living the Christian life is impossible without the Holy Spirit's help. This passage gives four reasons why we should relinquish control of our life to the Holy Spirit. First, he helps us make the right decisions if we listen to his advice. Second, he gives us the power to live by God's guidelines. Third, when we live by the Holy Spirit, he develops godly qualities—the fruit of the Spirit— in our life. Fourth, the Holy Spirit encourages us to seek God's approval above the approval of other people. In essence, the Holy Spirit enables Christians to live lives that are pleasing to God—something that is impossible to do on our own. He makes following Christ a joy rather than a duty.

Who Is Satan?

What is Satan, also known as Lucifer or the devil, like? Does he really look like the red-suited, pitchfork-holding cartoon caricature seated on a throne in hell? Or does he roam through the earth disguised as an angel of light? Unfortunately, far too many people do not have an accurate view of who Satan is. Many underestimate him and his prowess, even going as far as to doubt his very existence. The Bible clearly shows us just how active and conniving Satan really is. At the same time, Scripture also lets us know about Satan's limitations and ultimate demise. The more we understand the tactics of this intelligent spirit being, the better equipped we will be to ward off his attacks.

What Are Satan's Abilities?

2 CORINTHIANS 4:3-7

³If the Good News we preach is veiled from anyone, it is a sign that they are perishing. ⁴Satan, the god of this evil world, has blinded the minds of those who don't believe, so they are unable to see the glorious light of the Good News

that is shining upon them. They don't understand the message we preach about the glory of Christ, who is the exact likeness of God.

⁵We don't go around preaching about ourselves; we preach Christ Jesus, the Lord. All we say about ourselves is that we are your servants because of what Jesus has done for us. ⁶For God, who said, "Let there be light in the darkness," has made us understand that this light is the brightness of the glory of God that is seen in the face of Jesus Christ.

⁷But this precious treasure—this light and power that now shine within us—is held in perishable containers, that is, in our weak bodies.* So everyone can see that our glorious power is from God and is not our own.

4:7 Greek *But we have this treasure in earthen vessels.*

INSIGHTS FOR LIFE:

Ever since Satan lost his heavenly privileges, he has been using his abilities to oppose God's redeeming work among people. Paul's second letter to the Corinthians reveals at least three of Satan's abilities. First, he is the temporary god of this world, evidenced by the increasing wickedness around us. Second, Satan blinds the minds of unbelievers. He wants to keep unbelievers from getting to know God. Third, Satan is a master counterfeiter. One of Satan's greatest abilities is deception, making lies look like the truth. Since Satan has the power to do certain things in this world, we need to take steps to guard against his power and deception.

What Are Satan's Limitations?

JOB 1:1–2:10

¹There was a man named Job who lived in the land of Uz. He was blameless, a man of complete integrity. He feared God and stayed away from evil. . . .

⁶One day the angels* came to present themselves before the LORD, and Satan the Accuser came with them. ⁷"Where have you come from?" the LORD asked Satan.

And Satan answered the LORD, "I have been going back and forth across the earth, watching everything that's going on."

⁸Then the LORD asked Satan, "Have you noticed my servant Job? He is the finest man in all the earth—a man of complete integrity. He fears God and will have nothing to do with evil."

⁹Satan replied to the LORD, "Yes, Job fears God, but not without good reason! ¹⁰You have always protected him and his home and his property from harm. You have made him prosperous in everything he does. Look how rich he is! ¹¹But take away everything he has, and he will surely curse you to your face!"

¹²"All right, you may test him," the LORD said to Satan. "Do whatever you want with everything he possesses, but don't harm him physically." So Satan left the LORD's presence.

¹³One day when Job's sons and daughters were dining at the oldest brother's house, ¹⁴a messenger arrived at Job's home with this news: "Your oxen were plowing, with the donkeys feeding beside them, ¹⁵when the Sabeans raided us. They stole all the animals and killed all the farmhands. I am the only one who escaped to tell you."

¹⁶While he was still speaking, another messenger arrived with this news: "The fire of God has fallen from heaven and burned up your sheep and all the shepherds. I am the only one who escaped to tell you."

¹⁷While he was still speaking, a third messenger arrived with this news: "Three bands of Chaldean raiders have

1:6 Hebrew *the sons of God.*

stolen your camels and killed your servants. I am the only one who escaped to tell you."

¹⁸While he was still speaking, another messenger arrived with this news: "Your sons and daughters were feasting in their oldest brother's home. ¹⁹Suddenly, a powerful wind swept in from the desert and hit the house on all sides. The house collapsed, and all your children are dead. I am the only one who escaped to tell you."

²⁰Job stood up and tore his robe in grief. Then he shaved his head and fell to the ground before God. ²¹He said,

"I came naked from my mother's womb,
    and I will be stripped of everything when I die.
The LORD gave me everything I had,
    and the LORD has taken it away.
Praise the name of the LORD!"

²²In all of this, Job did not sin by blaming God.

²:¹One day the angels* came again to present themselves before the LORD, and Satan the Accuser came with them. ²"Where have you come from?" the LORD asked Satan.

And Satan answered the LORD, "I have been going back and forth across the earth, watching everything that's going on."

³Then the LORD asked Satan, "Have you noticed my servant Job? He is the finest man in all the earth—a man of complete integrity. He fears God and will have nothing to do with evil. And he has maintained his integrity, even though you persuaded me to harm him without cause."

⁴Satan replied to the LORD, "Skin for skin—he blesses you only because you bless him. A man will give up everything

2:1 Hebrew *the sons of God.*

he has to save his life. ⁵But take away his health, and he will surely curse you to your face!"

⁶"All right, do with him as you please," the LORD said to Satan. "But spare his life." ⁷So Satan left the LORD's presence, and he struck Job with a terrible case of boils from head to foot.

⁸Then Job scraped his skin with a piece of broken pottery as he sat among the ashes. ⁹His wife said to him, "Are you still trying to maintain your integrity? Curse God and die."

¹⁰But Job replied, "You talk like a godless woman. Should we accept only good things from the hand of God and never anything bad?" So in all this, Job said nothing wrong.

INSIGHTS FOR LIFE:
For all of his apparent abilities, Satan does not come close to equaling God's power. As this passage points out, Satan has definite limitations. First, while he can freely move throughout the earth, he cannot be in more than one place at one time. Second, though Satan does have certain abilities, his power is limited. Satan could not force Job to break under his attacks. Third, Satan is limited in what he can do in the life of a believer. Before Satan could do anything to Job, he had to seek God's permission. While Satan was allowed by God to destroy Job's servants and children, steal Job's goods, and strike Job with a sickness, God still kept a hedge of protection around him.

How Does Satan Attack?
GENESIS 3:1-19
¹Now the serpent was the shrewdest of all the creatures the LORD God had made. "Really?" he asked the woman. "Did God really say you must not eat any of the fruit in the garden?"

²"Of course we may eat it," the woman told him. ³"It's

only the fruit from the tree at the center of the garden that we are not allowed to eat. God says we must not eat it or even touch it, or we will die."

⁴"You won't die!" the serpent hissed. ⁵"God knows that your eyes will be opened when you eat it. You will become just like God, knowing everything, both good and evil."

⁶The woman was convinced. The fruit looked so fresh and delicious, and it would make her so wise! So she ate some of the fruit. She also gave some to her husband, who was with her. Then he ate it, too. ⁷At that moment, their eyes were opened, and they suddenly felt shame at their nakedness. So they strung fig leaves together around their hips to cover themselves.

⁸Toward evening they heard the LORD God walking about in the garden, so they hid themselves among the trees. ⁹The LORD God called to Adam,* "Where are you?"

¹⁰He replied, "I heard you, so I hid. I was afraid because I was naked."

¹¹"Who told you that you were naked?" the LORD God asked. "Have you eaten the fruit I commanded you not to eat?"

¹²"Yes," Adam admitted, "but it was the woman you gave me who brought me the fruit, and I ate it."

¹³Then the LORD God asked the woman, "How could you do such a thing?"

"The serpent tricked me," she replied. "That's why I ate it."

¹⁴So the LORD God said to the serpent, "Because you have done this, you will be punished. You are singled out from all the domestic and wild animals of the whole earth to be cursed. You will grovel in the dust as long as you live, crawling along on your belly. ¹⁵From now on, you and the woman will be enemies, and your offspring

3:9 Hebrew *the man,* and so throughout this chapter.

and her offspring will be enemies. He will crush your head, and you will strike his heel."

¹⁶Then he said to the woman, "You will bear children with intense pain and suffering. And though your desire will be for your husband,* he will be your master."

¹⁷And to Adam he said, "Because you listened to your wife and ate the fruit I told you not to eat, I have placed a curse on the ground. All your life you will struggle to scratch a living from it. ¹⁸It will grow thorns and thistles for you, though you will eat of its grains. ¹⁹All your life you will sweat to produce food, until your dying day. Then you will return to the ground from which you came. For you were made from dust, and to the dust you will return."

3:16 Or *And though you may desire to control your husband.*

INSIGHTS FOR LIFE:
Satan masterfully uses manipulation and distortion to deceive people. In this passage Satan tempts humans for the first time, providing information about his tactics. He used four ploys to lead Eve into sin. First, Satan questioned God's Word. He did not deny that God had spoken but simply questioned whether God had really said what Eve thought he had said. Second, Satan questioned God's love. He wanted to make Eve think that God was holding something back. Third, Satan denied God's Word. He went from "Did God really say this?" to "That's a lie!" Fourth, Satan substituted his own lie. Satan led Eve to believe that if she ate of the tree, she would become like God. The best defense against Satan's attack is to know what God says in his Word. Then we will be ready to defend against Satan's deception.

What Are Heaven and Hell?

The death of our physical body will bring us to one of two destinations—heaven or hell. From the Bible we know that heaven is a wonderful place, where the streets appear to be made of gold, and where pain, fear, and sorrow are no longer present. The Bible also tells us that hell is as terrible as heaven is wonderful. Interestingly, an increasing number of people believe in a place called hell, but most of them don't believe they are headed there. They think that hell is reserved only for hardened criminals. But the Scriptures tell us that people are not sent to hell for being bad any more than they are sent to heaven for being good. We all are sinful and deserve to spend eternity in hell (Romans 3:22-23). Those who reject the salvation offered through Jesus Christ will spend eternity in this place of torment.

What Is Heaven Like?
REVELATION 7:9-17
⁹After this I saw a vast crowd, too great to count, from every nation and tribe and people and language, standing in front of the throne and before the Lamb. They were clothed

in white and held palm branches in their hands. ¹⁰And they were shouting with a mighty shout, "Salvation comes from our God on the throne and from the Lamb!"

¹¹And all the angels were standing around the throne and around the elders and the four living beings. And they fell face down before the throne and worshiped God. ¹²They said,

"Amen! Blessing and glory and wisdom
and thanksgiving and honor and power and strength
belong to our God forever and forever. Amen!"

¹³Then one of the twenty-four elders asked me, "Who are these who are clothed in white? Where do they come from?"

¹⁴And I said to him, "Sir, you are the one who knows."

Then he said to me, "These are the ones coming out of the great tribulation. They washed their robes in the blood of the Lamb and made them white. ¹⁵That is why they are standing in front of the throne of God, serving him day and night in his Temple. And he who sits on the throne will live among them and shelter them. ¹⁶They will never again be hungry or thirsty, and they will be fully protected from the scorching noontime heat. ¹⁷For the Lamb who stands in front of the throne will be their Shepherd. He will lead them to the springs of life-giving water. And God will wipe away all their tears."

INSIGHTS FOR LIFE:

The apostle Paul had a taste of heaven, and in describing his experience, he said, "I was caught up into paradise" (2 Corinthians 12:2-4). The word paradise literally means "the royal garden of a king with all kinds of fruits and flowers." This passage in Revelation reveals four aspects of life in paradise. First, we will live without fear and worry. Heaven is a place of

*safety and protection (verse 15). Second, we will live without
need. Heaven is a place of complete sufficiency (verse 16).
Third, we will live without pain. Heaven is a place of comfort
(verse 16). Fourth, we will live without sorrow. Heaven is a
place of boundless joy (verse 17). In heaven we will be free of
life's cares and filled with the joy of being in God's presence.*

What Is Hell Like?
LUKE 16:19-31

[19]Jesus said, "There was a certain rich man who was splendidly clothed and who lived each day in luxury. [20]At his door lay a diseased beggar named Lazarus. [21]As Lazarus lay there longing for scraps from the rich man's table, the dogs would come and lick his open sores. [22]Finally, the beggar died and was carried by the angels to be with Abraham.* The rich man also died and was buried, [23]and his soul went to the place of the dead.* There, in torment, he saw Lazarus in the far distance with Abraham.

[24]"The rich man shouted, 'Father Abraham, have some pity! Send Lazarus over here to dip the tip of his finger in water and cool my tongue, because I am in anguish in these flames.'

[25]"But Abraham said to him, 'Son, remember that during your lifetime you had everything you wanted, and Lazarus had nothing. So now he is here being comforted, and you are in anguish. [26]And besides, there is a great chasm separating us. Anyone who wanted to cross over to you from here is stopped at its edge, and no one there can cross over to us.'

[27]"Then the rich man said, 'Please, Father Abraham, send him to my father's home. [28]For I have five brothers, and I

16:22 Greek *into Abraham's bosom.*   16:23 Greek *to Hades.*

want him to warn them about this place of torment so they won't have to come here when they die.'

²⁹"But Abraham said, 'Moses and the prophets have warned them. Your brothers can read their writings anytime they want to.'

³⁰"The rich man replied, 'No, Father Abraham! But if someone is sent to them from the dead, then they will turn from their sins.'

³¹"But Abraham said, 'If they won't listen to Moses and the prophets, they won't listen even if someone rises from the dead.' "

INSIGHTS FOR LIFE:
In this story, Jesus gave us a rare glimpse of hell, revealing some important facts about this dark place of punishment. First, a person's lifestyle in death will not be the same as it was in life. For the rich man, things dramatically changed for the worse when he passed into eternity. Second, hell is a place of flames and torment. The rich man in this story experienced unrelenting heat and an unquenchable thirst. Third, people do not "have a good time" in hell. Some people say, "I want to go to hell. All of my friends will be there." That may be true, but hell holds no parties. We don't need a tabloid account of a near-death experience to show us what hell is like; the Bible tells us all we need to know.

Who Will Enter Heaven?
JOHN 14:1-11

¹"Don't be troubled. You trust God, now trust in me. ²There are many rooms in my Father's home, and I am going to prepare a place for you. If this were not so, I would tell you plainly. ³When everything is ready, I will come and get you, so that you will always be with me

where I am. ⁴And you know where I am going and how to get there."

⁵"No, we don't know, Lord," Thomas said. "We haven't any idea where you are going, so how can we know the way?"

⁶Jesus told him, "I am the way, the truth, and the life. No one can come to the Father except through me. ⁷If you had known who I am, then you would have known who my Father is.* From now on you know him and have seen him!"

⁸Philip said, "Lord, show us the Father and we will be satisfied."

⁹Jesus replied, "Philip, don't you even yet know who I am, even after all the time I have been with you? Anyone who has seen me has seen the Father! So why are you asking to see him? ¹⁰Don't you believe that I am in the Father and the Father is in me? The words I say are not my own, but my Father who lives in me does his work through me. ¹¹Just believe that I am in the Father and the Father is in me. Or at least believe because of what you have seen me do.

14:7 Some manuscripts read *If you really have known me, you will know who my Father is.*

INSIGHTS FOR LIFE:

Hollywood often depicts the gates of heaven as the place where you "plead your case" for the right to enter. In this passage, Jesus clearly explains that the only ones who will enter heaven are those who have accepted him as the way, the truth, and the life—not those who have the best "arguments" or who have performed the most good deeds. Heaven is not a court but a prepared place for prepared people. Those who believe in Jesus Christ can rest assured that their reservation for heaven has been made. And when it comes to accommodations, we need not worry, for Jesus himself has promised to prepare a place for us.

Forgiveness

One of the great principles of the Christian life is forgiveness. Jesus modeled this principle for us when he hung on the cross and prayed for the very people who had put him there. His words were so powerful and unexpected that they brought about the conversion of one of the thieves hanging on a cross next to him. Because Jesus completely forgave us, he wants us to follow his example by forgiving others. As Scripture says, "Be kind to each other, tenderhearted, forgiving one another, just as God through Christ has forgiven you. Follow God's example in everything you do, because you are his dear children" (Ephesians 4:32–5:1).

Forgiveness Should Have No Limits
MATTHEW 18:21-35

²¹Then Peter came to him and asked, "Lord, how often should I forgive someone who sins against me? Seven times?"

²²"No!" Jesus replied, "seventy times seven!*

²³"For this reason, the Kingdom of Heaven can be com-

18:22 Or 77 times.

pared to a king who decided to bring his accounts up to date with servants who had borrowed money from him. ²⁴In the process, one of his debtors was brought in who owed him millions of dollars.* ²⁵He couldn't pay, so the king ordered that he, his wife, his children, and everything he had be sold to pay the debt. ²⁶But the man fell down before the king and begged him, 'Oh, sir, be patient with me, and I will pay it all.' ²⁷Then the king was filled with pity for him, and he released him and forgave his debt.

²⁸"But when the man left the king, he went to a fellow servant who owed him a few thousand dollars.* He grabbed him by the throat and demanded instant payment. ²⁹His fellow servant fell down before him and begged for a little more time. 'Be patient and I will pay it,' he pleaded. ³⁰But his creditor wouldn't wait. He had the man arrested and jailed until the debt could be paid in full.

³¹"When some of the other servants saw this, they were very upset. They went to the king and told him what had happened. ³²Then the king called in the man he had forgiven and said, 'You evil servant! I forgave you that tremendous debt because you pleaded with me. ³³Shouldn't you have mercy on your fellow servant, just as I had mercy on you?' ³⁴Then the angry king sent the man to prison until he had paid every penny.

³⁵"That's what my heavenly Father will do to you if you refuse to forgive your brothers and sisters in your heart."

18:24 Greek *10,000 talents.*　**18:28** Greek *100 denarii.* A denarius was the equivalent of a full day's wage.

INSIGHTS FOR LIFE:
The religious leaders of Jesus' day taught that those who had been wronged were to forgive someone two or three times—at the most! In this passage, Peter wondered if forgiving someone seven times would be enough from Jesus' perspective.

Imagine Peter's shock when Jesus told him that he should forgive up to "seventy times seven"—490 times. Does this mean that we should deny forgiveness on the 491st offense? Of course not. Rather, Jesus was teaching that we should extend unlimited forgiveness to others. We, as sinners, have been forgiven much. So we ought to forgive those who have hurt us, no matter how badly. They owe us little compared to what we once owed God.

Forgiveness Is Not Selective
MATTHEW 5:38-48

³⁸"You have heard that the law of Moses says, 'If an eye is injured, injure the eye of the person who did it. If a tooth gets knocked out, knock out the tooth of the person who did it.'* ³⁹But I say, don't resist an evil person! If you are slapped on the right cheek, turn the other, too. ⁴⁰If you are ordered to court and your shirt is taken from you, give your coat, too. ⁴¹If a soldier demands that you carry his gear for a mile,* carry it two miles. ⁴²Give to those who ask, and don't turn away from those who want to borrow.

⁴³"You have heard that the law of Moses says, 'Love your neighbor'* and hate your enemy. ⁴⁴But I say, love your enemies!* Pray for those who persecute you! ⁴⁵In that way, you will be acting as true children of your Father in heaven. For he gives his sunlight to both the evil and the good, and he sends rain on the just and on the unjust, too. ⁴⁶If you love only those who love you, what good is that? Even corrupt tax collectors do that much. ⁴⁷If you are kind only to your friends, how are you different from anyone

5:38 Greek *'An eye for an eye and a tooth for a tooth.'* Exod 21:24; Lev 24:20; Deut 19:21. 5:41 Greek *milion* [4,854 feet or 1,478 meters]. 5:43 Lev 19:18.
5:44 Some manuscripts add *Bless those who curse you, do good to those who hate you.*

else? Even pagans do that. [48]But you are to be perfect, even as your Father in heaven is perfect."

INSIGHTS FOR LIFE:
As one Bible commentator said, "To return evil for good is devilish; to return good for good is human. To return good for evil is divine." Although we are not divine, we, as believers, do not have the liberty to choose whom we will forgive or not forgive. We must do as Jesus has commanded and not only forgive our enemies, but love them as well. Loving our enemies does not come easily, but it is what Jesus calls us to do. It was Jesus himself who gave us the ultimate example of what it means to forgive our enemies. While hanging on the cross, he prayed, "Father, forgive these people because they don't know what they are doing" (Luke 23:34). God's Spirit has the power to enable us to love, pray, and do good to those who hate us.

Love

On one occasion Jesus was asked what commandment was the most important. He replied, "The most important commandment is this: 'Hear, O Israel! The Lord our God is the one and only Lord. And you must love the Lord your God with all your heart, all your soul, all your mind, and all your strength.' The second is equally important: 'Love your neighbor as yourself' " (Mark 12:29-31). If we truly love God with all our heart, soul, mind, and strength, we will want to follow all his other commands. In the same way, if we really love others as much as we love ourself, we will be concerned for their welfare and treat them accordingly. But before we can effectively love God, we must first realize how much he loves us. Scripture explains that God showed his great love for us by sending Christ to die for us while we were still sinners (Romans 5:8). The more we realize this wonderful truth, the more our love for God will grow. Our love for God comes as a result of his first loving us (1 John 4:19).

God Should Be the Greatest Love of Our Life
DEUTERONOMY 6:1-9

¹"These are all the commands, laws, and regulations that the LORD your God told me to teach you so you may obey

them in the land you are about to enter and occupy, ²and so you and your children and grandchildren might fear the LORD your God as long as you live. If you obey all his laws and commands, you will enjoy a long life. ³Listen closely, Israel, to everything I say. Be careful to obey. Then all will go well with you, and you will have many children in the land flowing with milk and honey, just as the LORD, the God of your ancestors, promised you.

⁴"Hear, O Israel! The LORD is our God, the LORD alone.* ⁵And you must love the LORD your God with all your heart, all your soul, and all your strength. ⁶And you must commit yourselves wholeheartedly to these commands am giving you today. ⁷Repeat them again and again to your children. Talk about them when you are at home and when you are away on a journey, when you are lying down and when you are getting up again. ⁸Tie them to your hands as a reminder, and wear them on your forehead. ⁹Write them on the doorposts of your house and on your gates."

6:4 Or *The* LORD *our God is one* LORD, or *The* LORD *our God, the* LORD *is one,* or *The* LORD *is our God, the* LORD *is one.*

INSIGHTS FOR LIFE:
The word used for love in these verses primarily speaks of an act of mind and will. It speaks of a committed, covenant love, not a love driven by transient, shallow emotion. Jesus spoke of this love when he quoted verse 5 to a lawyer who had asked him, "Teacher, which is the most important commandment in the law of Moses?" Speaking of this command from Deuteronomy, Jesus added, "This is the first and greatest commandment" (Matthew 22:37-38). If we love God with all of our heart, soul, and mind, the rest of God's commands will come naturally. Love for God is the basis for all obedience. Make a commitment today to truly love God—not with some temporary short-lived emotion, but with lasting wholehearted devotion.

Love Is the Greatest of All Spiritual Gifts
1 CORINTHIANS 13:1-13

¹If I could speak in any language in heaven or on earth*
but didn't love others, I would only be making meaningless
noise like a loud gong or a clanging cymbal. ²If I had the gift
of prophecy, and if I knew all the mysteries of the future and
knew everything about everything, but didn't love others,
what good would I be? And if I had the gift of faith so that I
could speak to a mountain and make it move, without love
I would be no good to anybody. ³If I gave everything I have
to the poor and even sacrificed my body, I could boast about
it;* but if I didn't love others,
I would be of no value whatsoever.

⁴Love is patient and kind. Love is not jealous or boastful
or proud ⁵or rude. Love does not demand its own way. Love
is not irritable, and it keeps no record of when it has been
wronged. ⁶It is never glad about injustice but rejoices whenever the truth wins out. ⁷Love never gives up, never loses
faith, is always hopeful, and endures through every circum-
stance.

⁸Love will last forever, but prophecy and speaking in
unknown languages* and special knowledge will all disappear. ⁹Now we know only a little, and even the gift of
prophecy reveals little! ¹⁰But when the end comes, these
special gifts will all disappear.

¹¹It's like this: When I was a child, I spoke and thought and
reasoned as a child does. But when I grew up, I put away
childish things. ¹²Now we see things imperfectly as in a
poor mirror, but then we will see everything with perfect
clarity.* All that I know now is partial and incomplete, but

13:1 Greek *in tongues of people and angels.* 13:3 Some manuscripts read *and even
gave my body to be burned.* 13:8 Or *in tongues.* 13:12 Greek *see face to face.*

then I will know everything completely, just as God knows me now.

¹³There are three things that will endure—faith, hope, and love—and the greatest of these is love.

INSIGHTS FOR LIFE:

This passage gives one of the most complete descriptions of love in the Bible. More important, it shows that love needs to be the one thing in life we seek more than anything else. Without it, whatever we do or say really has no lasting value. Here God says that love is patient, kind, unselfish, and faithful. This is a far cry from the love we see in our world—a love that is impatient, rude, selfish, and temporary. The kind of love God wants us to give others is impossible to manufacture on our own. You might say that it is a "supernatural" love. It is the natural outflow of God's presence in our life. That is why the Bible says, "[God] has given us the Holy Spirit to fill our hearts with his love" (Romans 5:5).

Joy

One noticeable change that takes place in a new believer's life is the inner joy he or she receives. In fact, joy is listed as a fruit of the Spirit that should be evident in every believer's life (Galatians 5:22). But this joy is different from the fleeting and temporary "happiness" that is usually dependent upon "good things" happening in someone's life. While sorrows will certainly come our way, the Holy Spirit gives us an inner joy and peace that cannot be taken away. Below are some of the ways we can experience God's joy in life.

Studying God's Word Helps Us Experience His Joy

NEHEMIAH 8:2-18

²So on October 8* Ezra the priest brought the scroll of the law before the assembly, which included the men and women and all the children old enough to understand. ³He faced the square just inside the Water Gate from early morning until noon and read aloud to everyone who

8:2 Hebrew *on the first day of the seventh month,* of the Hebrew calendar. This event occurred on October 8, 445 B.C.; also see note on 1:1.

could understand. All the people paid close attention to the Book of the Law. [4]Ezra the scribe stood on a high wooden platform that had been made for the occasion. To his right stood Mattithiah, Shema, Anaiah, Uriah, Hilkiah, and Maaseiah. To his left stood Pedaiah, Mishael, Malkijah, Hashum, Hashbaddanah, Zechariah, and Meshullam. [5]Ezra stood on the platform in full view of all the people. When they saw him open the book, they all rose to their feet.

[6]Then Ezra praised the LORD, the great God, and all the people chanted, "Amen! Amen!" as they lifted their hands toward heaven. Then they bowed down and worshiped the LORD with their faces to the ground.

[7]Now the Levites—Jeshua, Bani, Sherebiah, Jamin, Akkub, Shabbethai, Hodiah, Maaseiah, Kelita, Azariah, Jozabad, Hanan, and Pelaiah—instructed the people who were standing there. [8]They read from the Book of the Law of God and clearly explained the meaning of what was being read, helping the people understand each passage. [9]Then Nehemiah the governor, Ezra the priest and scribe, and the Levites who were interpreting for the people said to them, "Don't weep on such a day as this! For today is a sacred day before the LORD your God." All the people had been weeping as they listened to the words of the law.

[10]And Nehemiah* continued, "Go and celebrate with a feast of choice foods and sweet drinks, and share gifts of food with people who have nothing prepared. This is a sacred day before our Lord. Don't be dejected and sad, for the joy of the LORD is your strength!"

[11]And the Levites, too, quieted the people, telling them, "Hush! Don't weep! For this is a sacred day." [12]So the people went away to eat and drink at a festive meal, to

8:10 Hebrew *he.*

share gifts of food, and to celebrate with great joy because they had heard God's words and understood them.

¹³On October 9* the family leaders and the priests and Levites met with Ezra to go over the law in greater detail. ¹⁴As they studied the law, they discovered that the LORD had commanded through Moses that the Israelites should live in shelters during the festival to be held that month.* ¹⁵He had said that a proclamation should be made throughout their towns and especially in Jerusalem, telling the people to go to the hills to get branches from olive, wild olive, myrtle, palm, and fig trees. They were to use these branches to make shelters in which they would live during the festival, as it was prescribed in the law.

¹⁶So the people went out and cut branches and used them to build shelters on the roofs of their houses, in their courtyards, in the courtyards of God's Temple, or in the squares just inside the Water Gate and the Ephraim Gate. ¹⁷So everyone who had returned from captivity lived in these shelters for the seven days of the festival, and everyone was filled with great joy! The Israelites had not celebrated this way since the days of Joshua son of Nun. ¹⁸Ezra read from the Book of the Law of God on each of the seven days of the festival. Then on October 15* they held a solemn assembly, as the law of Moses required.

8:13 Hebrew *On the second day,* of the seventh month of the Hebrew calendar. This event occurred on October 9, 445 B.C.; also see notes on 1:1 and 8:2.
8:14 Hebrew *in the seventh month.* This month of the Hebrew lunar calendar usually occurs in September and October. See Lev 23:39-43.   8:18 Hebrew *on the eighth day,* of the seventh month of the Hebrew calendar. This event occurred on October 15, 445 B.C.; also see notes on 1:1 and 8:2.

INSIGHTS FOR LIFE:
As we read this account, we see how the study of God's Word should lead to joy. Simply reading the Bible and studying its contents is not enough. Several other things must also take

*place. We must make the study of God's Word a priority
(verses 1-5). Our study of God's Word should lead to worship
(verse 6). We need to take time to understand what passages
mean (verses 7-8). We need to rejoice about what we have
learned and share it with others (verses 9-12). We need to
apply what we have learned (verses 13-18). As we study,
understand, and obey God's Word, it produces joy in our life.
And that joy of the Lord will be our strength, carrying us
through the trials of life.*

Knowing and Trusting God Brings Great Joy
1 PETER 1:3-9

³All honor to the God and Father of our Lord Jesus Christ,
for it is by his boundless mercy that God has given us the
privilege of being born again. Now we live with a wonderful
expectation because Jesus Christ rose again from the dead.
⁴For God has reserved a priceless inheritance for his children. It is kept in heaven for you, pure and undefiled,
beyond the reach of change and decay. ⁵And God, in his
mighty power, will protect you until you receive this salvation, because you are trusting him. It will be revealed on the
last day for all to see. ⁶So be truly glad!* There is wonderful
joy ahead, even though it is necessary for you to endure
many trials for a while.

⁷These trials are only to test your faith, to show that it is
strong and pure. It is being tested as fire tests and purifies
gold—and your faith is far more precious to God than mere
gold. So if your faith remains strong after being tried by fiery
trials, it will bring you much praise and glory and honor on
the day when Jesus Christ is revealed to the whole world.

⁸You love him even though you have never seen him.

1:6 Or *So you are truly glad.*

Though you do not see him, you trust him; and even now you are happy with a glorious, inexpressible joy. ⁹Your reward for trusting him will be the salvation of your souls.

INSIGHTS FOR LIFE:

Many people today are seeking joy and happiness but not finding it. Perhaps they don't understand what true happiness is. At best, they only find fleeting happiness can be found in possessions, pleasures, or accomplishments. But the joy God gives is not just some emotional feeling. It is not affected by our circumstances. In fact, it is an unchanging, natural by-product of our faith in Jesus Christ. As you trust in Jesus and look forward to his return, you will be filled with an "inexpressible joy." It won't be just some sort of emotional high. It will be a deep, supernatural experience of contentedness based upon the fact that your life is right with God. And this lasting joy and happiness will sustain you for the rest of your life.

Peace

Peace of mind—it seems almost elusive in a day when murders are commonplace, job security is nonexistent, and the moral fabric of society is falling apart. Yet Jesus has promised that each one of us can experience true peace: "I am leaving you with a gift—peace of mind and heart! And the peace I give isn't fragile like the peace the world gives. So don't be troubled or afraid" (John 14:27). Unfortunately, some people are so caught up in the "pursuit of peace," that they have forgotten that Jesus has already given it to them. They have simply left that gift "unopened." And we cannot find peace outside of the parameters God has given us. As Augustine said many years ago, "Our souls are restless until they find their rest in God." Begin to "unwrap" this precious gift by examining what God's Word has to say about it.

Peace Begins When We Give Our Life to God
MATTHEW 11:25-30

²⁵Then Jesus prayed this prayer: "O Father, Lord of heaven and earth, thank you for hiding the truth from those who

think themselves so wise and clever, and for revealing it to the childlike. ²⁶Yes, Father, it pleased you to do it this way!

²⁷"My Father has given me authority over everything. No one really knows the Son except the Father, and no one really knows the Father except the Son and those to whom the Son chooses to reveal him."

²⁸Then Jesus said, "Come to me, all of you who are weary and carry heavy burdens, and I will give you rest. ²⁹Take my yoke upon you. Let me teach you, because I am humble and gentle, and you will find rest for your souls. ³⁰For my yoke fits perfectly, and the burden I give you is light."

INSIGHTS FOR LIFE:

In this passage, Jesus teaches us three things we must do in order to find true peace or "rest." First, we need to come to Jesus. Those who have accepted Jesus Christ as Lord and Savior have already taken this step. Those who are still searching might be right at the door. But know this: True peace cannot be found in any other way. Second, we must exchange our yoke for his yoke. A yoke is a wooden harness placed across the shoulders of oxen so they can pull something. We need to remove the heavy yoke of sin and put on the lighter yoke of God's gracious forgiveness. Third, we need to let Jesus lead. This is hard because we want to be in control. But to find rest we must give God the reins so he can "teach" us.

God's Peace Needs to Rule in Our Heart
COLOSSIANS 3:12-17

¹²Since God chose you to be the holy people whom he loves, you must clothe yourselves with tenderhearted mercy, kindness, humility, gentleness, and patience. ¹³You must make allowance for each other's faults and forgive the person who offends you. Remember, the Lord forgave you, so you must forgive others. ¹⁴And the most important piece of

clothing you must wear is love. Love is what binds us all together in perfect harmony. ¹⁵And let the peace that comes from Christ rule in your hearts. For as members of one body you are all called to live in peace. And always be thankful.

¹⁶Let the words of Christ, in all their richness, live in your hearts and make you wise. Use his words to teach and counsel each other. Sing psalms and hymns and spiritual songs to God with thankful hearts. ¹⁷And whatever you do or say, let it be as a representative of the Lord Jesus, all the while giving thanks through him to God the Father.

INSIGHTS FOR LIFE:

One of the important marks of the Christian is peace. As Paul points out in verse 15, the peace of a Christian comes from Christ and "rules" in the heart. Christ's peace should act as an "umpire" or judge in our life, deciding our outlook no matter what the circumstances. What is Christ's peace like? It is not anxious about anything but trusts God (Philippians 4:6-7). It doesn't doubt that God is in control (Mark 4:35-41). It doesn't forget God's blessings and answers to prayer (Philippians 4:6). It should be present in our relationships (Psalm 34:14). It comes from Christ alone (John 16:33). It is produced by the Holy Spirit (Galatians 5:22). It promotes peace with others (James 3:18). Give God your worries and concerns, and ask him to replace them with his peace.

Purity

Purity is a quality we hear too little about today. Usually when we do hear something about purity, it is in reference to sexual purity. But purity goes beyond this to include wholesome thoughts, a sincere desire to do what is right, and a commitment to obey God's Word. Jesus alluded to the importance of purity by promising that those whose hearts were pure would see God (Matthew 5:8). In using the word *heart*, Jesus was saying that the center of our being—our will, our emotions, and our thought processes—needs to be cleansed of sin. The following Bible passages examine the idea of purity and how it affects us as followers of Jesus Christ.

Avoid Situations of Temptation
2 SAMUEL 11:1–12:12

¹The following spring, the time of year when kings go to war, David sent Joab and the Israelite army to destroy the Ammonites. In the process they laid siege to the city of Rabbah. But David stayed behind in Jerusalem.

²Late one afternoon David got out of bed after taking a nap and went for a stroll on the roof of the palace. As he

looked out over the city, he noticed a woman of unusual beauty taking a bath. ³He sent someone to find out who she was, and he was told, "She is Bathsheba, the daughter of Eliam and the wife of Uriah the Hittite." ⁴Then David sent for her; and when she came to the palace, he slept with her. (She had just completed the purification rites after having her menstrual period.) Then she returned home. ⁵When Bathsheba discovered that she was pregnant, she sent a message to inform David.

⁶So David sent word to Joab: "Send me Uriah the Hittite." ⁷When Uriah arrived, David asked him how Joab and the army were getting along and how the war was progressing. ⁸Then he told Uriah, "Go on home and relax." David even sent a gift to Uriah after he had left the palace. ⁹But Uriah wouldn't go home. He stayed that night at the palace entrance with some of the king's other servants.

¹⁰When David heard what Uriah had done, he summoned him and asked, "What's the matter with you? Why didn't you go home last night after being away for so long?"

¹¹Uriah replied, "The Ark and the armies of Israel and Judah are living in tents,* and Joab and his officers are camping in the open fields. How could I go home to wine and dine and sleep with my wife? I swear that I will never be guilty of acting like that."

¹²"Well, stay here tonight," David told him, "and tomorrow you may return to the army." So Uriah stayed in Jerusalem that day and the next. ¹³Then David invited him to dinner and got him drunk. But even then he couldn't get Uriah to go home to his wife. Again he slept at the palace entrance.

¹⁴So the next morning David wrote a letter to Joab and gave it to Uriah to deliver. ¹⁵The letter instructed Joab,

11:11 Or *at Succoth.*

"Station Uriah on the front lines where the battle is fiercest. Then pull back so that he will be killed." [16]So Joab assigned Uriah to a spot close to the city wall where he knew the enemy's strongest men were fighting. [17]And Uriah was killed along with several other Israelite soldiers.

[18]Then Joab sent a battle report to David. [19]He told his messenger, "Report all the news of the battle to the king. [20]But he might get angry and ask, 'Why did the troops go so close to the city? Didn't they know there would be shooting from the walls? [21]Wasn't Gideon's son Abimelech killed* at Thebez by a woman who threw a millstone down on him?' Then tell him, 'Uriah the Hittite was killed, too.' "

[22]So the messenger went to Jerusalem and gave a complete report to David. [23]"The enemy came out against us," he said. "And as we chased them back to the city gates, [24]the archers on the wall shot arrows at us. Some of our men were killed, including Uriah the Hittite."

[25]"Well, tell Joab not to be discouraged," David said. "The sword kills one as well as another! Fight harder next time, and conquer the city!"

[26]When Bathsheba heard that her husband was dead, she mourned for him. [27]When the period of mourning was over, David sent for her and brought her to the palace, and she became one of his wives. Then she gave birth to a son. But the LORD was very displeased with what David had done.

[12:1]So the LORD sent Nathan the prophet to tell David this story: "There were two men in a certain town. One was rich, and one was poor. [2]The rich man owned many sheep and cattle. [3]The poor man owned nothing but a little lamb he had worked hard to buy. He raised that little lamb, and it grew up with his children. It ate from the man's own plate

11:21 Hebrew *Was not Abimelech son of Jerubbesheth killed.*

and drank from his cup. He cuddled it in his arms like a baby daughter. ⁴One day a guest arrived at the home of the rich man. But instead of killing a lamb from his own flocks for food, he took the poor man's lamb and killed it and served it to his guest."

⁵David was furious. "As surely as the LORD lives," he vowed, "any man who would do such a thing deserves to die! ⁶He must repay four lambs to the poor man for the one he stole and for having no pity."

⁷Then Nathan said to David, "You are that man! The LORD, the God of Israel, says, 'I anointed you king of Israel and saved you from the power of Saul. ⁸I gave you his house and his wives and the kingdoms of Israel and Judah. And if that had not been enough, I would have given you much, much more. ⁹Why, then, have you despised the word of the LORD and done this horrible deed? For you have murdered Uriah and stolen his wife. ¹⁰From this time on, the sword will be a constant threat to your family, because you have despised me by taking Uriah's wife to be your own.

¹¹" 'Because of what you have done, I, the LORD, will cause your own household to rebel against you. I will give your wives to another man, and he will go to bed with them in public view. ¹²You did it secretly, but I will do this to you openly in the sight of all Israel.' "

INSIGHTS FOR LIFE:

David fell into temptation without thinking of the consequences. His spiritual descent was even more perplexing because he was "a man after God's own heart." In this account, David made four common mistakes that led to his failure. First, David lowered his guard. Instead of leading his troops into battle, or spending time with God in worship, he was idle. Second, David entertained the temptation. When David saw Bathsheba bathing, he could have turned away but didn't. Third, David acted upon the temptation. He could have repented and stopped there, but he went ahead with the immoral relationship. Fourth, David developed a dullness toward sin. When David found out that Bathsheba was pregnant, instead of making things right, he committed other sins. Learn from David's tragic mistake. Know your weaknesses and avoid situations where temptation might overcome you.

If You Fall, Ask for Forgiveness
PSALM 51:1-19

For the choir director: A psalm of David, regarding the time Nathan the prophet came to him after David had committed adultery with Bathsheba.

¹ Have mercy on me, O God,
   because of your unfailing love.
  Because of your great compassion,
   blot out the stain of my sins.
² Wash me clean from my guilt.
   Purify me from my sin.

³ For I recognize my shameful deeds—
   they haunt me day and night.
⁴ Against you, and you alone, have I sinned;
   I have done what is evil in your sight.
  You will be proved right in what you say,
   and your judgment against me is just.

⁵ For I was born a sinner—
   yes, from the moment my mother conceived me.
⁶ But you desire honesty from the heart,
   so you can teach me to be wise in my inmost
     being.

⁷Purify me from my sins,* and I will be clean;
  wash me, and I will be whiter than snow.
⁸Oh, give me back my joy again;
  you have broken me—
  now let me rejoice.
⁹Don't keep looking at my sins.
  Remove the stain of my guilt.
¹⁰Create in me a clean heart, O God.
  Renew a right spirit within me.
¹¹Do not banish me from your presence,
  and don't take your Holy Spirit from me.
¹²Restore to me again the joy of your salvation,
  and make me willing to obey you.
¹³Then I will teach your ways to sinners,
  and they will return to you.
¹⁴Forgive me for shedding blood, O God who saves;
  then I will joyfully sing of your forgiveness.
¹⁵Unseal my lips, O Lord,
  that I may praise you.

¹⁶You would not be pleased with sacrifices,
  or I would bring them.
 If I brought you a burnt offering,
  you would not accept it.
¹⁷The sacrifice you want is a broken spirit.
  A broken and repentant heart, O God,
  you will not despise.

¹⁸Look with favor on Zion and help her;
  rebuild the walls of Jerusalem.
¹⁹Then you will be pleased with worthy sacrifices
  and with our whole burnt offerings;
  and bulls will again be sacrificed on your altar.

51:7 Hebrew *Purify me with the hyssop branch.*

David wrote this psalm after being confronted by Nathan about his affair with Bathsheba. David had not confessed his sin to God for a full year—and what a miserable year it had been! He wrote, "There was a time when I wouldn't admit what a sinner I was. My dishonesty made me miserable and filled my days with frustration. All day and all night your hand was heavy on me. My strength evaporated like water on a sunny day" (Psalm 32:3-4). Like David, we will be miserable until we confess our sins. Then we must also ask God to help purify our heart. David recognized the wickedness of his heart and realized he needed help to change. If you have already sinned, turn to God now for his forgiveness. Only God can forgive you, restore your joy, and fill you with the right desires.

Beware of the Sins of the Heart
MATTHEW 5:17-30

¹⁷"Don't misunderstand why I have come. I did not come to abolish the law of Moses or the writings of the prophets. No, I came to fulfill them. ¹⁸I assure you, until heaven and earth disappear, even the smallest detail of God's law will remain until its purpose is achieved. ¹⁹So if you break the smallest commandment and teach others to do the same, you will be the least in the Kingdom of Heaven. But anyone who obeys God's laws and teaches them will be great in the Kingdom of Heaven.

²⁰"But I warn you—unless you obey God better than the teachers of religious law and the Pharisees do, you can't enter the Kingdom of Heaven at all!

²¹"You have heard that the law of Moses says, 'Do not murder. If you commit murder, you are subject to judgment.'*

5:21 Exod 20:13; Deut 5:17.

²²But I say, if you are angry with someone,* you are subject to judgment! If you say to your friend, 'You idiot,'* you are in danger of being brought before the court. And if you curse someone,* you are in danger of the fires of hell.

²³"So if you are standing before the altar in the Temple, offering a sacrifice to God, and you suddenly remember that someone has something against you, ²⁴leave your sacrifice there beside the altar. Go and be reconciled to that person. Then come and offer your sacrifice to God. ²⁵Come to terms quickly with your enemy before it is too late and you are dragged into court, handed over to an officer, and thrown in jail. ²⁶I assure you that you won't be free again until you have paid the last penny.

²⁷"You have heard that the law of Moses says, 'Do not commit adultery.'* ²⁸But I say, anyone who even looks at a woman with lust in his eye has already committed adultery with her in his heart. ²⁹So if your eye—even if it is your good eye*—causes you to lust, gouge it out and throw it away. It is better for you to lose one part of your body than for your whole body to be thrown into hell. ³⁰And if your hand—even if it is your stronger hand*—causes you to sin, cut it off and throw it away. It is better for you to lose one part of your body than for your whole body to be thrown into hell."

5:22a Some manuscripts add *without cause.* 5:22b Literally *'Raca,'* an Aramaic term of contempt. 5:22c Greek *if you say, 'You fool.'* 5:27 Exod 20:14; Deut 5:18. 5:29 Greek *your right eye.* 5:30 Greek *your right hand.*

INSIGHTS FOR LIFE:
Jesus tells us here that even a lustful glance is as sinful as committing adultery. This goes far beyond the demands of today's morality. Jesus' remedy for this problem—gouging out the eye—seems rather harsh. But in essence, he is saying that we should be willing to give up whatever is necessary to keep us

from falling into sin. That may mean terminating a relationship, canceling a cable channel or magazine subscription, or changing how we spend our spare time. In other words, we need to avoid things that have a spiritually destructive effect on our life. Then we can take practical steps to fill our mind with the things of God (see Philippians 4:8).

Discernment

An inspector who worked for Scotland Yard in the counterfeit department was once asked if he spent a lot of time handling counterfeit money. He said, "No." He then explained that he spent so much time handling the real thing that he could immediately detect the counterfeit. In the same way, as we become knowledgeable about God's Word, we, too, will be able to detect teachings and concepts that are contrary to the teachings of Scripture. Make no mistake—counterfeit "truth" is out there in force. The following Scripture passages should give us hints about how to keep from falling prey to false teachings.

Beware of Satan's Clever Imitations
MATTHEW 13:24-30

²⁴Here is another story Jesus told: "The Kingdom of Heaven is like a farmer who planted good seed in his field. ²⁵But that night as everyone slept, his enemy came and planted weeds among the wheat. ²⁶When the crop began to grow and produce grain, the weeds also grew. ²⁷The farmer's

servants came and told him, 'Sir, the field where you planted that good seed is full of weeds!'

²⁸" 'An enemy has done it!' the farmer exclaimed.

" 'Shall we pull out the weeds?' they asked.

²⁹"He replied, 'No, you'll hurt the wheat if you do. ³⁰Let both grow together until the harvest. Then I will tell the harvesters to sort out the weeds and burn them and to put the wheat in the barn.' "

INSIGHTS FOR LIFE:

This is known as the parable of the wheat and the weeds. Jesus gave this illustration to expose the satanic tactic of imitation and infiltration. In the initial stages of growth, the weeds looked similar to the wheat. But in time the weed grows and shows itself for what it really is—a plant that will impede the growth of the wheat. In essence, Satan often follows the pattern of planting weed seed in his attacks against the church. He has "flooded the market" with false teachings—imitations of the real thing. Satan knows that half-truths are usually more dangerous than blatant lies. We must guard against falling for gospel imitations at all cost.

Use God's Word to Evaluate Someone's Teachings

ACTS 17:10-15

¹⁰That very night the believers sent Paul and Silas to Berea. When they arrived there, they went to the synagogue. ¹¹And the people of Berea were more open-minded than those in Thessalonica, and they listened eagerly to Paul's message. They searched the Scriptures day after day to check up on Paul and Silas, to see if they were really teaching the truth.

¹²As a result, many Jews believed, as did some of the prominent Greek women and many men.

¹³But when some Jews in Thessalonica learned that Paul was preaching the word of God in Berea, they went there and stirred up trouble. ¹⁴The believers acted at once, sending Paul on to the coast, while Silas and Timothy remained behind. ¹⁵Those escorting Paul went with him to Athens; then they returned to Berea with a message for Silas and Timothy to hurry and join him.

INSIGHTS FOR LIFE:
The group of people in this passage—the Bereans—searched the written Word of God to see if Paul's words were true. They did this because they knew that they could trust God's Word and use it as the standard against which to evaluate the teachings of others. The same is true for us today. Everything we need to know about God is found in the pages of Scripture. Applying ourselves in the study of his Word helps us determine whether someone's teachings are true or false. If we fail to study the Bible, we may be lured into believing false teachings. But if we consistently study God's Word, it— along with the illumination of the Holy Spirit—will enable us to distinguish truth from error.

Know the Difference between Truth and Falsehood
1 JOHN 4:1-6
¹Dear friends, do not believe everyone who claims to speak by the Spirit. You must test them to see if the spirit they have comes from God. For there are many false prophets in the world. ²This is the way to find out if they have the Spirit of God: If a prophet acknowledges that Jesus Christ

became a human being, that person has the Spirit of God. ³If a prophet does not acknowledge Jesus, that person is not from God. Such a person has the spirit of the Antichrist. You have heard that he is going to come into the world, and he is already here.

⁴But you belong to God, my dear children. You have already won your fight with these false prophets, because the Spirit who lives in you is greater than the spirit who lives in the world. ⁵These people belong to this world, so they speak from the world's viewpoint, and the world listens to them. ⁶But we belong to God; that is why those who know God listen to us. If they do not belong to God, they do not listen to us. That is how we know if someone has the Spirit of truth or the spirit of deception.

INSIGHTS FOR LIFE:

False teachings are not unique to our times. When the apostle John wrote this passage, a false teaching called Gnosticism was popular. It taught that Jesus was a mere human being and claimed that "the Christ" came upon Jesus at his baptism and left him before his crucifixion. Of course this was false, yet this heresy is still taught by some today. We need to "test" any such teachings to see if they really come from God. Any attempt to cast doubt upon the Bible's sufficiency should be rejected. Any "broadness" that admits another way to God outside of Christ is false. Anytime Jesus Christ is reduced to one of many gods or prophets it is erroneous. The best way to know the false is to be familiar with the true: God's Word, the Bible.

Perseverance

There will be times in our Christian walk when we will feel emotionally "down." We may think that God has forgotten about us. Or we might become discouraged as we see others who have believed in Jesus Christ lose interest and fall away. We may wonder whether we are next on the devil's "hit list." But God will not allow us to be hit with more than we can handle spiritually. In fact, it is during times of trouble that we will actually be strengthened, not weakened. As we read the Bible, we will come across words like *endurance* and *perseverance*. These words are often used when the Bible compares the Christian life to a race. The race referred to is a marathon, not a fifty-yard dash. Because the Christian life is a long-distance run, we need to pace ourself, to persevere, and most of all, to *finish* the race.

Life's Trials Will Make Us Stronger
JAMES 1:2-18

²Dear brothers and sisters, whenever trouble comes your way, let it be an opportunity for joy. ³For when your faith is tested, your endurance has a chance to grow. ⁴So let it grow,

for when your endurance is fully developed, you will be strong in character and ready for anything.

⁵If you need wisdom—if you want to know what God wants you to do—ask him, and he will gladly tell you. He will not resent your asking. ⁶But when you ask him, be sure that you really expect him to answer, for a doubtful mind is as unsettled as a wave of the sea that is driven and tossed by the wind. ⁷People like that should not expect to receive anything from the Lord. ⁸They can't make up their minds. They waver back and forth in everything they do.

⁹Christians who are* poor should be glad, for God has honored them. ¹⁰And those who are rich should be glad, for God has humbled them. They will fade away like a flower in the field. ¹¹The hot sun rises and dries up the grass; the flower withers, and its beauty fades away. So also, wealthy people will fade away with all of their achievements.

¹²God blesses the people who patiently endure testing. Afterward they will receive the crown of life that God has promised to those who love him. ¹³And remember, no one who wants to do wrong should ever say, "God is tempting me." God is never tempted to do wrong, and he never tempts anyone else either. ¹⁴Temptation comes from the lure of our own evil desires. ¹⁵These evil desires lead to evil actions, and evil actions lead to death. ¹⁶So don't be misled, my dear brothers and sisters.

¹⁷Whatever is good and perfect comes to us from God above, who created all heaven's lights.* Unlike them, he never changes or casts shifting shadows. ¹⁸In his goodness he chose to make us his own children by giving us his true word. And we, out of all creation, became his choice possession.

1:9 Greek *The brother who is.*   1:17 Greek *from above, from the Father of lights.*

One of the keys to growing and being able to effectively continue in the Christian life is enduring. A key aspect of endurance is patience. This cheerful, enduring patience, which helps us to continue in our Christian walk, actually comes—and develops— in times of testing and hardship. During these "storms of life," our spiritual roots grow deeper, thus strengthening our faith. If we had our way, most of us would probably try to avoid these difficult times. Yet God promises that he will never give us more than we can handle (1 Corinthians 10:13). These times of trial and testing will either make us better or bitter. It really is up to us and the outlook we choose to take. We should not view difficulties as obstacles to our faith, but as opportunities for spiritual growth.

Christ Endured Great Pain for Us
HEBREWS 12:1-13

¹Therefore, since we are surrounded by such a huge crowd of witnesses to the life of faith, let us strip off every weight that slows us down, especially the sin that so easily hinders our progress. And let us run with endurance the race that God has set before us. ²We do this by keeping our eyes on Jesus, on whom our faith depends from start to finish.* He was willing to die a shameful death on the cross because of the joy he knew would be his afterward. Now he is seated in the place of highest honor beside God's throne in heaven. ³Think about all he endured when sinful people did such terrible things to him, so that you don't become weary and give up. ⁴After all, you have not yet given your lives in your struggle against sin.

⁵And have you entirely forgotten the encouraging words God spoke to you, his children? He said,

12:2 Or *Jesus, the Originator and Perfecter of our faith.*

"My child, don't ignore it when the Lord disciplines you,
      and don't be discouraged when he corrects you.
   [6] For the Lord disciplines those he loves,
      and he punishes those he accepts as his children."*

[7]As you endure this divine discipline, remember that God is treating you as his own children. Whoever heard of a child who was never disciplined? [8]If God doesn't discipline you as he does all of his children, it means that you are illegitimate and are not really his children after all. [9]Since we respect our earthly fathers who disciplined us, should we not all the more cheerfully submit to the discipline of our heavenly Father and live forever*?

[10]For our earthly fathers disciplined us for a few years, doing the best they knew how. But God's discipline is always right and good for us because it means we will share in his holiness. [11]No discipline is enjoyable while it is happening—it is painful! But afterward there will be a quiet harvest of right living for those who are trained in this way.

[12]So take a new grip with your tired hands and stand firm on your shaky legs. [13]Mark out a straight path for your feet. Then those who follow you, though they are weak and lame, will not stumble and fall but will become strong.

12:5-6 Prov 3:11-12.

INSIGHTS FOR LIFE:
Jesus modeled the ultimate in endurance so that we would be encouraged to keep our faith strong in the race of life. Throughout the New Testament, the Christian life is compared to a race. With that in mind, we need to realize that it is not a short sprint, but a long-distance run. Sometimes, as we are participating in this race, we can grow discouraged by circumstances or by what others say to us. But just as a successful

runner must "keep his eyes on the prize," we, too, must remember what this race is all about. We must bear in mind for whom and to whom we are running: Jesus Christ. In essence, we need to keep our eyes on Jesus.

How You Can Know God

What's Missing in Our Life?
Purpose, meaning, a reason for living—these are all
things we desire and search for in life. But despite our
search, we still feel empty and unfulfilled. We each have
an empty place in our heart, a spiritual void, a "God-
shaped vacuum." Possessions won't fill it, nor will suc-
cess, relationships, or even religion. Only through a
vibrant relationship with God can this void be filled, but
before such a relationship can be established, we need
to face a serious problem.

The Problem: Sin
The Bible identifies this problem as sin. Sin is not just the
bad things we do but an inherent part of who we are. We
are not sinners because we sin; we sin because we are
sinners. King David once wrote, "I was born a sinner—yes,
from the moment my mother conceived me" (Psalm
51:5). Because we are born sinners, sinning comes to us
naturally. Scripture tells us, "The human heart is most
deceitful and desperately wicked. Who really knows how
bad it is?" (Jeremiah 17:9). Every problem we experience
in society today can be traced back to our refusal to live
God's way.

The Solution: Jesus Christ
God understood our problem and knew we could not
beat it alone. So he lovingly sent his own Son, Jesus
Christ, to bridge the chasm of sin that separates us from

God. Jesus laid aside his divine privileges and walked the earth as a man, experiencing all the troubles and emotions that we do. Then he was arrested on false charges and killed on a Roman cross. But this was no accident. He did it to suffer the punishment deserved by us all. And then three days later, Jesus rose from the dead, conquering sin and death forever!

The Response: Accepting God's Offer

To know Jesus Christ personally and have our sins forgiven, we must believe that we are sinners separated from God and that our only hope is Jesus Christ, the Son of God, who came and died for our sins. But we must not stop with this realization. We also need to take steps toward confessing and turning from our sins. And we must welcome Jesus Christ into our life as Lord and Savior. He will move in and help us to change from the inside out.

If you are ready to repent of your sins and believe in Jesus Christ so that you can receive his forgiveness, take a moment to pray like this:

God, I'm sorry for my sins. Right now, I turn from my sins and ask you to forgive me. Thank you for sending Jesus Christ to die on the cross for my sins. Jesus, I ask you to come into my life and be my Lord, Savior, and Friend. Thank you for forgiving me and giving me eternal life. In Jesus' name I pray, amen.

If you prayed this prayer and meant it, you can be sure that God has forgiven you and received you into his family.

If you have enjoyed reading the Bible passages presented in *Cornerstones for Living*, you can experience the entire text of the New Living Translation through any one of these quality editions:

DELUXE TEXT EDITION
The *Holy Bible*, Deluxe Text Edition, is perfect for anyone who wishes to experience God's Word through the New Living Translation. It features clear, easy-to-read type and a beautiful, long-lasting binding.

LIFE APPLICATION STUDY BIBLE
This best-selling study Bible contains over 10,000 Life Application™ notes to help you apply the truth of God's Word to everyday life.

TOUCHPOINT BIBLE
The *TouchPoint Bible* quickly directs you to specific passages in God's Word on hundreds of topics you are most likely to face.

NEW BELIEVER'S BIBLE

The *New Believer's Bible* presents the basics of Christianity in a way that is easy to follow and understand. Also available in a New Testament edition.

THE ONE YEAR BIBLE

Through a simple and easy-to-use format, *The One Year Bible* gives you an organized method of reading through the entire Bible in one year!

BIBLE ON CASSETTE

The beauty and style of the New Living Translation comes alive through this dramatic, multivoice presentation.